THE SNUGGLE IS REAL

THE SNUGGLE IS REAL

A HAVE A LITTLE PUN COLLECTION

BY FRIDA CLEMENTS

CHRONICLE BOOKS

SAN FRANCISCO

LIBRARY OF CONGRESS CATALOGING-IN-PUBLICATION DATA AVAILABLE.

ISBN 978-1-4521-7137-1

MANUFACTURED IN CHINA

ILLUSTRATIONS AND LETTERING BY FRIDA CLEMENTS.
LAYOUT BY KAYLA FERRIERA.

10 9 8 7 6 5 4 3 2 1

CHRONICLE BOOKS LLC
680 SECOND STREET
SAN FRANCISCO, CALIFORNIA 94107

www.chroniclebooks.com

"*If at first the idea isn't absurd, then there's no hope for it.*"
— Albert Einstein

"Wit and puns aren't just décor in the mind; they're essential signs that the mind knows it's on, recognizes its own software, can spot the bugs in its own program."
— Adam Gopnik

"A DAY WITHOUT LAUGHTER IS A DAY WASTED."
— CHARLIE CHAPLIN

INTRODUCTION

I don't know what is wrong (or right) with my brain, but I seem to always be playing with words and making funny connections. On a visit to Iceland, I was astounded by the majestic beauty of the waterfalls, but also giggled as I thought to myself "I Mist You." Later on in the day, as I listened to the tour guide discuss the history of elves in Icelandic culture, I mused "Talk Amongst Your Elves." Last Thanksgiving, in the midst of prepping a casserole, I said "You're Doing Grate!" to a large block of cheese.

Puns get a bad rap, and I totally get it. A terrible pun is the worst. But occasionally, they make you giggle like a five year old, or give you an "aha" moment you've never considered before. Those are my favorite. Thinking of puns can also be very cathartic for the not-so-great aspects of life. They have helped console me when I have to wake up early ("I'm in Morning"), and also capture how I really feel about the saxophone ("This Blows"). Or if a task seems nearly impossible, I can tell myself, you gotta "Stick with It," and "Just Be Leaf."

Up until I started illustrating these puns (and publishing my first book, HAVE A LITTLE PUN), I had considered myself more of a serious artist. My illustrations have been featured on posters for touring bands, in advertising, books, and many other projects, and I still love to create nature-inspired screen prints. However, my true personality is probably more semi-serious. Humor is definitely how I make it through the day to day, and these puns are a fun way to blend my love of detailed illustration with my silly and slightly irreverent side.

When I first started illustrating puns, I called my strange new hobby "puncrastinating." Obsessing over crumpled lists of words lying around the house and coming up with cute little drawings was a fun way to give myself a break from more serious client projects, folding laundry, or any of the countless tasks one does in a day. In fact, keeping my mind busy on puns made the grunt work a lot more fun! I also love that these little illustrations seem to make people happy (smile, giggle, or groan, I'll take it). Have a little pun!

JUST BE LEAF

YOU GO, GRILL

KEEPIN' IT WHEEL

BEAR
WITH ME

EVERY BUNNY
NEEDS
SOME
BUNNY

WEAVE IT
TO ME

MINT TO BE

THAT'S WHAT
CHEESE SAID

DON'T OVERDUE IT

IT'S ALL GEEK TO ME

DARN IT

OH MY GOURD

LET'S GET KRAKEN

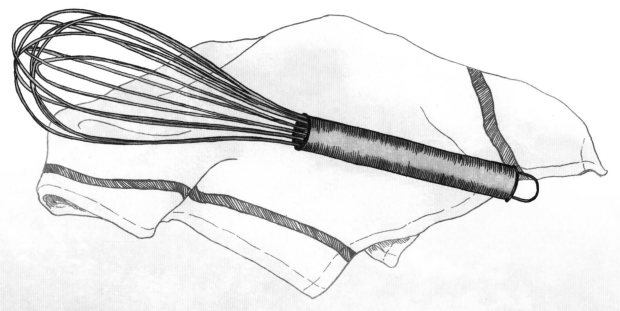

GIVE PEAS
A CHANCE

YOU'RE A PEELING

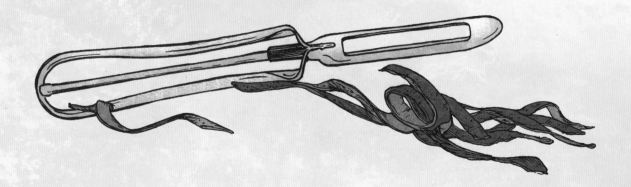

I YAM WHAT I YAM

SOFA SO GOOD

I'M A BIG FAN

MUMS THE WORD

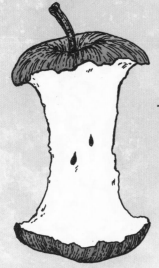

WORKING
ON MY CORE

THISTLE DO

MOO
LA LA

TALK AMONGST YOUR ELVES

SEAL THE DEAL

TOLLED YOU!

THIS
BLOWS

GET TO
THE PINT

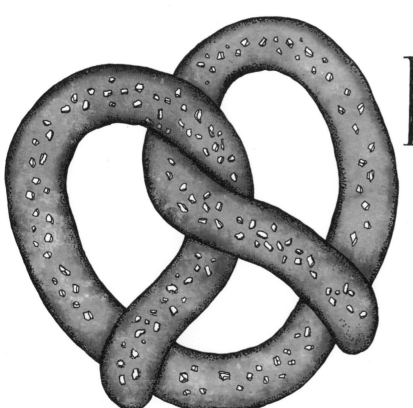

WHAT A
TWIST

SAKÉ TO ME

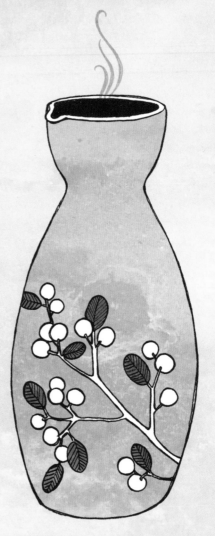

LET'S ROLL

I'M IN MORNING

ESPRESSO YOURSELF

DONUT DISTURB

THE SNUGGLE IS REAL

WHAT DO RHINO?

CURRANT OBSESSION

I'M A LITTLE HORSE

I AIN'T LION

I POD

NECK
AND
NECK

I EGRET NOTHING

IRIS
MY CASE

ACKNOWLEDGMENTS

THANKS TO MY DEAR HUSBAND, TOMO NAKAYAMA,
FOR HIS STEADFAST LOVE & SUPPORT.

THANKS TO ALL OF MY INCREDIBLE FRIENDS
AND FAMILY. YOU INSPIRE ME DAILY.

FINALLY, ETERNAL GRATITUDE TO STEVE MOCKUS
AND THE WONDERFUL FOLKS AT CHRONICLE BOOKS
FOR LETTING ME HAVE ALL THIS PUN!

DEDICATION

THIS BOOK IS FOR ANYONE WHO GETS THE JOKE,
FOR WE ARE KINDRED SPIRITS.
I CAN TELL BY THAT TWINKLE IN YOUR EYE.

ABOUT THE AUTHOR

Frida Clements is a Seattle-based illustrator particularly
known for her beautiful screen-printed poster designs.
When she's not drawing or puncrastinating, she enjoys
long walks in the woods, crosswords over brunch,
and dressing her dog in adorable sweaters.
See more of her work at fridaclements.com.